P9-AZX-890

On Morning Wings

On Morning Wings

Adapted from Psalm 139 by

Reeve Lindbergh

illustrated by

Holly Meade

CANDLEWICK PRESS
CAMBRIDGE, MASSACHUSETTS

Lord, you look at me and know me,
Every step I take, you show me.

When I rise, and when I rest,
You will always know me best.

Where I walk, or sit, or stand,
You still hold me in your hand.

And if I don't know how to pray,
You understand me, anyway.

Once when I was lost,
you found me.
Then I felt your arms
around me.

When I'm afraid and want to hide,
You are always by my side.

When I'm lonely, you are near,
When I'm angry, you stay here.

High as heaven bright, you greet me,
Down in darkness, too, you meet me.

You are with me everywhere:
In light and shadow, fire and air;

In every tiny grain of sand;
And in the desert, vast and grand;

On morning wings, in oceans deep;
When I'm awake, and when I sleep.

In my secret self, you made me,
In the blazing sun, you shade me.

Know me, lead me, guide my way

Through every hour of every day,
For all my life, in all I do,

I will always be with you.

In memory of my father and all who love wings
R. L.

Text copyright © 2002 by Reeve Lindbergh
Illustrations copyright © 2002 by Holly Meade

"On Morning Wings" was previously published in the anthology *In Every Tiny Grain of Sand: A Child's Book of Prayers and Praise*, collected by Reeve Lindbergh, published by Candlewick Press, 2000.

All rights reserved. No part of this book may be reproduced, transmitted, or stored in an information retrieval system in any form or by any means, graphic, electronic, or mechanical, including photocopying, taping, and recording, without prior written permission from the publisher.

First edition 2002

Library of Congress Cataloging-in-Publication Data

Lindbergh, Reeve.
On morning wings / adapted from Psalm 139
by Reeve Lindbergh ; illustrated by Holly Meade.
p.   cm.
Summary: Retells, in simple words, a psalm of
God's knowledge of and love for each of us.
ISBN 0-7636-1106-9
1. Bible. O.T. Psalms CXXXIX—Paraphrases, English—Juvenile literature.
[1. Bible. O.T. Psalms CXXXIX—Paraphrases. 2. God.]
I. Meade, Holly ill. II. Bible. O.T. Psalms CXXXIX. III. Title.
BS1450 1 39th L56 2002
223'.209505—dc21   2001058169

2 4 6 8 10 9 7 5 3 1

Printed in China

This book was typeset in Calligraphic.
The illustrations were done in watercolor and collage.

Candlewick Press
2067 Massachusetts Avenue
Cambridge, Massachusetts 02140

visit us at www.candlewick.com